CHURCHES OF THE NEW FOREST AND ITS BORDERS

by

Barry and Georgina Peckham

First published in 1994

Second Printing 1995

by NOVA FORESTA PUBLISHING

185 Lyndhurst Road, Ashurst, Southampton, SO40 7AR

Set in New Century Schoolbook

and printed by Frost Printers 01703 292960

ISBN 0 9523173 0 3

Front Cover : Minstead Church

Back Cover : Brockenhurst Church

CONTENTS

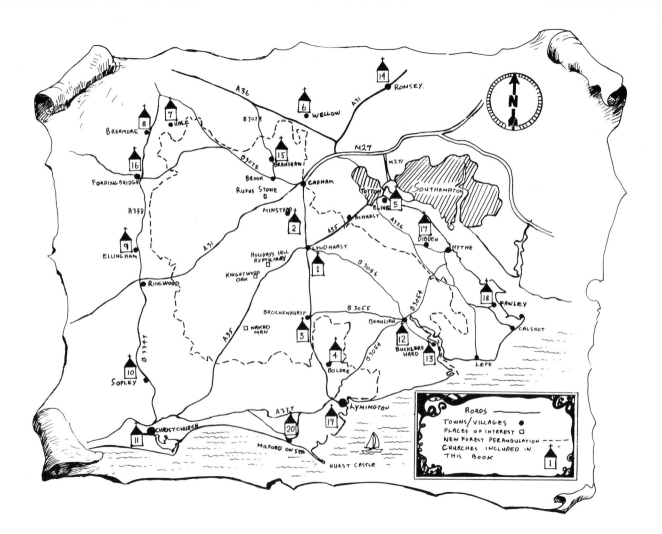

Introduction

The early chroniclers claimed that many churches were destroyed and villages laid waste when William I set aside the New Forest as a Royal Hunting Preserve, over 900 years ago. More recent historical evidence however, lends weight to the opinion that these early claims were grossly exaggerated. The infertile soil of the New Forest could not have sustained the amount of population that would be needed to fill so many churches. However, working on the premise that there is no smoke without fire, it is fairly safe to assume that at least some churches disappeared in this volatile period of our history. Fortunately the forest still abounds with fine examples of early church architecture.

The earliest churches featured in this book date from Saxon times and some are recorded in Domesday Book, while others owe much to the Victorian style of architecture. This book is, by no means, intended as a definitive guide to churches of the New Forest. We have selected what we feel are the most interesting by virtue of their antiquity, their connection with famous personalities and their proximity to places of general interest.

Georgina Peckham

Lyndhurst
St. Michael and All Angels

It would be difficult for any visitor to Lyndhurst to miss the Victorian church of St. Michael and All Angels standing as it does on an artificial mound overlooking the village. An exceptional example of the architecture of the period it was designed by William White in the early 1860s and was built using local brick with Bathstone dressings.

The church houses an outstanding fresco, painted by Frederick, Lord Leighton which tells the parable of the Wise and Foolish Virgins. Leighton painted it while staying with a friend at Lyndhurst in 1862 and he used local girls as models. It stands eight feet high and twenty-four feet long and occupies the whole of the wall space under the east window.

Also to be found in the church is a memorial to the two sons of Reginald and Alice Hargreaves who fell in the First World War. Alice Hargreaves (*née* Liddell) was the inspiration for Lewis Carroll's *Alice's Adventures in Wonderland*. She lived with her family at Cuffnells, a house near Lyndhurst which has since been demolished, and is buried in a simple family grave in the churchyard outside the South Transept.

Beyond the church lies the 17th century Queen's House — the New Forest Headquarters of the Forestry Commission — the Verderers' Hall and ancient Court Room. In the main car park is the New Forest Museum and Visitor Centre where the history and characters of the Forest can be seen and experienced.

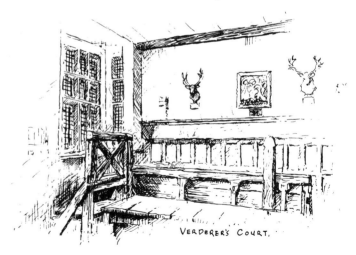

VERDERER'S COURT.

Minstead
All Saints

Reached by way of a small lane running between the green and the Trusty Servant inn, All Saints at Minstead is a quaint miscellany of architectural styles. The addition of galleries and private pews over the centuries, which led to the introduction of windows from different periods, has given the exterior an unusual 'homely' look.

The list of rectors dates from 1279 and the present church building is not mentioned before 1272 but parts of it are certainly earlier. A fine Gothic archway leads into the church from the North Porch and the 18th century tower, built of red and blue Hampshire brick, is topped by a pinnacle and gilded weather vane.

All Saints' crowning glory must be its almost unique collection of furniture and fittings. The rare 3-decker pulpit dates from the 17th century and the equally remarkable 'Squire's Pew' was a private pew built for the occupants of Castle Malwood, the large house a mile to the north-west. The pew resembles a sitting room with comfortable seats and a fireplace and was originally entered from the outside but the door is now sealed.

In the churchyard, under the branches of an oak, is the grave of the creator of Sherlock Holmes, Sir Arthur Conan Doyle and his wife Lady Jean. They were originally buried in the garden of their home "Windlesham" in Crowborough, Sussex but when the house was sold in 1953 their bodies were exhumed and re-interred at Minstead to be near their holiday home at Bignell Wood.

His epitaph reads "Steel True, Blade Straight, Arthur Conan Doyle, Knight, Patriot, Physician and Man of Letters". Minstead is featured in his book *The White Company* written in 1890. The oak tree bears evidence of having been struck by lightning three times since the grave was closed.

BIGNELL WOOD.

Brockenhurst
St. Nicholas

Brockenhurst is the only village mentioned in Domesday Book as having a church. The parish church of St. Nicholas is built on a mound a quarter of a mile south of the village. There is speculation as to whether the site may date back to pagan times and gives rise to its claim as 'the oldest church in the Forest'.

Built of flint with 18th century brick additions, the south doorway is one of the church's best features, giving evidence of late Norman architecture. Inside, the bowl of the font, lead-lined and fashioned from Purbeck Stone, dates from the 12th century.

In the churchyard, the Great Yew Tree which stands at the west end of the church, is possibly as old as the church, since its girth in 1793, was already fifteen feet!

You cannot fail to notice the impressive New Zealand Cemetery which commemorates soldiers who died in Brockenhurst hospitals during the First World War. The cemetery is situated on the east side of the churchyard, on the central level. Nearby is the grave of local eccentric and snake-catcher Harry 'Brusher' Mills.

Brusher lived in nearby Gritnam in a clotten hut and earned his living by selling snakes to London Zoo for a shilling a piece. He has become something of a symbol of the Forest, as any visitor to the New Forest Museum at Lyndhurst will discover. The pub in Brockenhurst village, formerly the Railway Inn, has been renamed in his honour.

Unfortunately, due to deliberate fire damage in 1975, the church is now kept locked except for Sunday Services and weekday afternoons between May and September when a member of the congregation will be pleased to welcome visitors.

Boldre
St. John the Baptist

A first time visitor to St. John's Church at Boldre may be surprised by its isolated hilltop position a fair distance from the village. This is by no means uncommon among the older Forest churches which were built at the centre of the parishes they served rather than existing villages.

Certainly, with open forest on one side and a cultivated valley rolling away on the other, few churches can claim a lovelier setting.

Recently celebrating its 900th anniversary, Boldre church retains features from the 11th century to the present day. You enter the church through the 13th century South Porch, but the upper portion of the squat brick tower was built as late as 1697. In the spacious and uncluttered interior you will see evidence of 14th century craftsmanship in the bosses and oak beams of the wagon roof.

From a list of the distinguished incumbents of St. John's, pride of place must go to William Gilpin, vicar from 1777 until his death, aged 80, in 1804. An accomplished artist and illustrator, Gilpin wrote *Remarks on Forest Scenery, and other Woodland Views*. Published in 1791 it was to become one of the foremost works on the forest landscape.

Gilpin also founded a poorhouse in the village and a 'model' school now called 'Gilpin's Cottage'. Gilpin's tomb can be found in the extensive churchyard to the north of the church.

The church contains the only memorial to HMS *Hood*. Sunk by the Bismarck in Icelandic waters in 1941, HMS *Hood* was the flagship of Vice-Admiral Holland who was a regular worshipper at St. John's.

An interesting entry in the parish register reveals the marriage of Robert Southey, Poet Laureate to the New Forest poet Caroline Bowles in 1839.

GILPIN'S TOMB

Eling
St. Mary's

In Southampton, during the mid 1600s, Isaac Watts, looking out across the river to Eling, was moved to write the hymn 'There is a land of pure delight'. Still, today, it is not difficult to recognise the source of his inspiration.

Eling is now a peaceful backwater but the church of St. Mary's gives evidence that it was once the centre of a much larger parish which included Netley Marsh, Copythorne, Colbury and Marchwood.

The port of Eling and Eling Wharf played an important part in ship-building history, owing its popularity to its position as a natural outlet to the sea from the eastern part of the Forest. Here timber cut for royal ships could be floated down river.

St. Mary's itself has a rather confused history. There is evidence of Saxon foundations but is mainly of 13th century architecture with extensive mid-Victorian restoration. The church houses a splendid example of 16th century Venetian painting in 'The Last Supper' probably an early work of Bonifazio or one of his assistants.

There are some notable epitaphs to be found in the churchyard and a path leading to Goatee Park where the best view of Eling Quay can be obtained.

At the bottom of the hill on which St. Mary's stands is Eling Mill and Toll House. The mill was restored in 1980 and opened to the public as a working Tide Mill Museum and is unique in Western Europe as the only mill which harnesses the power of the tide for flour production.

ELING MILL

East Wellow
St. Margaret of Antioch

The village of Wellow was presented by King Alfred to his daughter Ethelfreda — 'Lady of the Mercians'. Although tucked away, St. Margaret's is well signposted. Founded in the year the Magna Carta was signed — 1215 — the church boasts many original 13th century wall paintings including one of St. Christopher carrying the infant Christ across a stream and another depicting the murder of Thomas Becket.

There is an unusual timber belfry of the dovecote type and the ancient door, *circa* 850, still carries the holes where rats and other vermin were nailed in the 16th century.

The church also houses relics and mementoes of the Crimean War in commemoration of the renowned nurse and reformer Florence Nightingale. Florence lived in the family home of Embley Park in Wellow parish. She realised very early in life that her vocation was caring for the sick and as a 'gentlewoman' raised the status of nursing from the menial to an 'honourable' occupation. After reading, in 1854, of the terrible conditions in hospitals in the Crimea, she volunteered and arrived at Scutaria with 38 other nurses. Within two months she had transformed the working conditions and, on her feet for 20 hours a day, earned the title 'Lady with the Lamp' as she went about her nightly rounds. She died in 1910, aged 90 and is buried in St. Margaret's churchyard. At her own request her stone carries only her initials and dates.

In Ryedown Lane, a few yards from the crossroads south of Embley Park, there is a stone seat which once formed part of the 'Sounding Arch' bridge which connected two parts of the Embley estate. The bridge was frequently used by Florence and there is a legend in Wellow that her ghost can be seen riding, complete with carriage and horses, under the now demolished arch, every year on New Year's Eve.

SOUNDING ARCH SEAT

B.A. Pelham, 9?

Hale

St. Mary's

St. Mary's at Hale can be easily overlooked, nestling as it does on a wooded terrace above the River Avon, in the grounds of Hale Manor but its setting and unusual character add to the charm of this little church. Approached from the road it is quite a steep climb but it can also be reached by driving into the main entrance of Hale Manor, up the tree lined avenue from the lodge, where it is signposted and has its own car park.

The church was rebuilt in 1717 by the architect Thomas Archer who lived at Hale Park and is buried in the church. The oldest part of the fabric of the interior are the stone seats along the nave walls where the 'old' sat with their backs to the wall! In about 1766 the nave was tiled and probably replaced a thatched roof. The barrel roof was built in 1895 from wood grown on the Estate. The font is 14th century but was not ornamented until Tudor times.

The names of parishioners killed in the First World War are carved on the wooden Prie-dieu at the centre step to the chancel and in the chancel are two very impressive stained glass windows, on either side of the altar, depicting Joshua and St. Michael.

Only the grounds of Hale Park are open to the public as the Manor itself is privately occupied but a small diversion into Hale village and you will find Hatchet Green. At the west end of the green stands a thatched cottage, with porches and dormers, which in the 18th and 19th centuries was a 'Dame' school — the forerunner of our nursery schools. At the east end is a circular mound, called the Windmill Ball, which is almost certainly a Bronze Age barrow.

DAME SCHOOL.

Breamore

St. Mary's

Nestling in the Avon Valley, the village of Breamore is situated along the A338 between Fordingbridge and Downton. The Saxon church of St. Mary's lies a half mile or so west of the road. A visit to Breamore is a step back into another century. The village pond, ducks on the green and pretty cottages set apart give an open, spacious feel guaranteed to slow your pace.

The church, set in picturesque Breamore Park and surrounded by majestic trees, truly earns the title 'ancient' being built in *circa* A.D.980. It is one of the very few Hampshire churches to possess a Saxon Rood or Sculpture. The Rood, now badly mutilated, depicts Our Lady and St. John and the Manus Dei (hand of God) projecting downwards from the clouds. The archway leading to the South Transept bears a unique Anglo-Saxon inscription, probably dating from the reign of Ethelred II, which, in translation, reads 'Here is made plain the covenant to thee'.

The church is overlooked by the imposing Elizabethan Manor, Breamore House. If you visit the House and the adjoining Countryside and Carriage Museums don't miss the chance to see the ancient turf mizmaze a mile or so distant on Breamore Down. The maze is reached by way of a footpath through Breamore Wood, a pleasant if uphill walk. The origin of the maze is something of a mystery and controversy continues as to whether it was cut by Bronze Age people or Medieval Monks.

MIZMAZE

B.A. Peckham '93

Ellingham
St. Mary and All Saints

The delightful little church at Ellingham, with a dual dedication to St. Mary and All Saints, is tucked away at the end of a lane, off the A338, two miles from the market town of Ringwood.

The main fabric of the church dates from the 13th century but there are many examples of Georgian architecture as extensive restoration and rebuilding was carried out in 1746. Among these are the stone and red brick of the west wall and the entrance porch.

Over the porch, in the tympanum, is an impressive blue and gilt sundial which is still accurate to within five and a half minutes. A single bell, cast by Clement Tosier of Salisbury in 1712, is housed in the cedar shingled tower.

To the right of the entrance porch is the tomb of Lady Alice Lisle of Moyles Court who was condemned at the Bloody Assizes by the notorious Judge Jeffreys. Lady Lisle was accused of harbouring two men who were fleeing for their lives from the Monmouth rebellion. She was betrayed by a villager and arrested to be tried at Winchester. At first the blood thirsty Jeffreys ordered her to be burned alive but, after an outcry at the severity of the sentence, it was commuted to beheading!

SUNDIAL.

At nearby Ibsley, where the charming triple arched bridge affords distant views of the Avon valley, you can find, in the little church, the final resting place of Heywood Sumner the renowned New Forest artist and archaeologist.

B.A. PECKHAM '92

Sopley
St. Michael and All Angels

The little village of Sopley, near Christchurch, has one of the shortest one-way systems in Hampshire, with each of the streets being no more than 250 yards long.

Lying off a bend in the road to the south of the village, the church is beautifully positioned on a knoll overlooking the Avon Water Meadows and not far from the county boundary.

The church, dating from the 13th century, is mainly constructed of Ironstone rubble — probably obtained from Hengistbury Head a few miles away. At one time claimed by Breamore, it was proved that Sopley Church belonged to Christchurch Priory 'by perpetual right' and Breamore gave up their claim when Christchurch undertook to make a yearly payment of 40 lbs. of pure wax.

Do not miss the two very interesting corbels, at the west end, of angels playing a double pipe and a viol. Similar corbels are to be found in Christchurch Priory suggesting the same craftsman was employed in both cases.

The tombs of two brave soldiers — General George Willis and John, First Lord Keane are to be found in the churchyard.

The church overlooks Sopley Mill, which is now a restaurant, and the attractive sluice gates. Sopley forge is a working blacksmith's.

Nearby, at Avon Tyrrell, is the ford where Sir Walter Tyrrell reputedly crossed the Avon whilst fleeing from the scene of the mysterious death of King Rufus in 1100. It was near here that a blacksmith is said to have shod Tyrrell's horse during his flight and, until recent times, was required to pay an annual fine to the crown.

CORBEL.

Christchurch Priory

Legend has it that the church at Christchurch — then known as Twynham — was originally to be built on St. Catherine's Hill to the north of the town. Under cover of darkness the stones, which were carried to the hilltop each day, mysteriously disappeared and were found the next day on the promontory between the Avon and the Stour — the present site of the Priory.

Suspecting divine intervention the early builders set to work to build the church on the chosen spot and were joined by an unknown workman who would take neither food nor payment.

When the building was nearing completion it was discovered that a roof beam had been cut too short. The discouraged workmen retired and on their return found that not only was the beam the correct length but that it had been raised to its rightful position in the roof. The strange workman was not seen again and the early monks, considering that such help could only have come from Christ himself, renamed both the church and the town.

The 'Miraculous Beam' can still be seen and attracts visitors from all over the world.

The Priory also has the distinction of being the longest parish church in England and houses a massive Norman nave, four beautiful chantry chapels and an impressive 14th century Jesse screen.

Adjoining the Priory are the ruins of the Old Castle and the Norman House and it is only a short walk to the Quay and the ancient Place Mill which was mentioned in Domesday Book.

PLACE MILL

Beaulieu Abbey Church
Blessed Virgin and Child

Originally built as the Monks' Refectory to the Abbey, the church of the Blessed Virgin and Child at Beaulieu is probably unique among English parish churches as, according to the early Cistercian custom, it runs north to south.

The Abbey was founded by King John in A.D.1205 for the White Monks and he endowed it with lands and exempted it from the feudal tolls and taxes. More than a century later Pope Innocent received the Abbey into the protection of the apostolical see; giving the Cistercians immunity from secular and diocesan authority. They paid the price, however, when Henry VIII dissolved the Abbey in A.D.1538. Most of the buildings were destroyed, although the inner and outer gate-houses still remain, as do portions of the cloisters and the chapter house. The Refectory was allowed to stand in order to be used as the parish church.

The Beaulieu Cistercians were the subject of Conan Doyle's book *The White Company*.

Inside the church can be seen the Reader's Pulpit from which readings were given to the monks at meal times. The roof, with its painted bosses, probably dates from the 15th century.

Beaulieu, originally named Bella Locus and meaning 'beautiful place', certainly lives up to its name and offers much of interest to the visitor including riverside walks to nearby Buckler's Hard.

Entrance to the church from Beaulieu village is by arrangement during the morning or via the National Motor Museum in the afternoon.

THE CLOISTERS

Buckler's Hard
The Chapel of the Blessed Virgin Mary

Two miles from Beaulieu and lying on the western bank of the river is the quaint hamlet of Buckler's Hard. It was founded originally in the 18th century as a port for West Indian trade but is now better known as a former ship-building yard. At least four of Nelson's battleships, among them the *Agamemnon*, were built here and floated down the Beaulieu River to the Solent.

In the double row of cottages that border the green can still be found the Master Builder's House and situated between the Shipwright's Cottage and the Yachtsman's Bar is the Chapel of the Blessed Virgin Mary.

The chapel was, in the ship-building days, a cobbler's shop and later, the village dame's school. During the restoration and conversion work a smuggler's den was found in the cellar and is still intact.

The dark carved panelling in the interior comes from the dining hall at Lady Cross Lodge, a house in the New Forest. The wooden statue of the Virgin is French and over 300 years old. She stands on a wooden block which was formerly the chopping block of the monks of Beaulieu Abbey.

Buckler's Hard was the home port of Sir Francis Chichester's *Gipsy Moth* yachts and a wooden plaque in the chapel commemorates his achievements. It reads 'Sir Francis Chichester, K.B.E.. 1901-1972. Navigator of the skies and seas, Inspirer of the hearts of men'. The plaque was unveiled by Lord Montagu of Beaulieu on the 12th anniversary of Sir Francis' death.

The small but well appointed Maritime Museum is well worth a visit.

BEAULIEU RIVER

Romsey Abbey

Romsey Abbey is one of the largest and best examples of a Norman Conventual Church in existence. It was founded in A.D.907 by King Edward the Elder and his daughter Elfreda and was originally built as a nunnery.

The abbey was dissolved as a nunnery in 1539 and sold to the parishioners of Romsey in 1544 and has remained as the town's parish church ever since.

Inside the abbey, behind the choir screen on the north side, can be seen the remains of the Anglo-Saxon church which once stood on the site but the present building is over 850 years old. It is difficult to focus on particular treasures in the magnificent interior as the Abbey is so rich in rare antiquities but among them are the three-storey high Norman arches, a Saxon Rood behind the altar, 12th century wall paintings and 700 year old floor tiles, depicting the crusades, in front of the altar in St. George's Chapel.

Also to be found in the church is the final resting place of Admiral of the Fleet, Earl Mountbatten of Burma who lived at Broadlands, the elegant Palladian mansion on the outskirts of the town. Broadlands is open to the public and is set in superb surroundings on the banks of the Test.

There is hardly a street in the ancient market town of Romsey that does not contain at least one building of historical interest. King John's House and the adjoining Tudor cottage off Church Street and Bartlett's Almshouses, now in Abbey Meads but built originally in Middlebridge Street in 1807, are particularly notable.

A plaque in Bell Street states 'Body of King William Rufus carried through here on way to Winchester for burial'. It is supposed that William Purkis brought the King's body in his cart by the quickest route from the New Forest.

KING JOHNS HOUSE

B. A. Needham

Bramshaw

St. Peter's

To the north of the elongated village of Bramshaw, standing on high ground and overlooking the road, is the attractive church of St. Peter's. Village tradition has it that William Rufus stabled his horses in the church that stood on the site before the Norman Conquest. There is no evidence, sadly, to support this claim as the earliest recorded mention of the church is in 1158.

Extensive remodelling on the 12th and 13th century foundations took place in 1829 by one John Penistone, County Surveyor for Wiltshire: perhaps a man known for his thrift as an uprooted gatepost was used as a lintel over the main door under the tower.

Until the Act of 1895 St. Peter's had the curious distinction of having its nave in Wiltshire and its chancel in Hampshire.

There are two galleries inside the church; the West Gallery, converted in the 1860s as a family pew for the inhabitants of Bramble Hill House and the South Gallery, built for the girls' school with 'free sittings for the Females only'. In the South Transept is a memorial to seven members of the parish who went down with the *Titanic*.

Fordingbridge
St. Mary's

St. Mary's is mostly of the Early English period with an unusual 15th century addition. The tower, usually to be found at the West end of a church, was positioned over the centre of the North side because of the proximity of the road.

In the North chapel is a splendid example of a hammerbeam roof richly carved in chestnut and the East window of the chapel shows man's journey from earth to heaven.

The celebrated artist Augustus John lived a mile from Fordingbridge at Fryern Court, Upper Burgate. There is a statue of him by Ivor Roberts-Jones in Fordingbridge Park. John's Bohemian lifestyle brought him displeasure from the art establishment of the time but his talent is indisputable. He lived at Fryern Court until his death in 1961 and he is buried at the town cemetery on the Stuckton road.

Fawley
All Saints

The rubble walls and tiled roofs of All Saints give a pleasant look to this long and low village church. Although much restored, especially after bomb damage in the Second World War, it retains a great deal of its character. In fact, since the removal of the pews, due to dry rot, and the disappearance of the Victorian galleries the spacious interior probably looks much as it must have done centuries ago.

Restoration was carried out in 1954 by Randoll Blacking and he found in the fabric of the church a small round-headed window, supposedly Saxon and cut from a single piece of stone. This has been inserted into the external wall under the East window.

When a volcano erupted on Tristan da Cunha in 1961 the inhabitants of the island were evacuated to former Royal Air Force married quarters at Calshot and the church houses a model of one of their boats. The church plate includes an Elizabethan chalice.

Flight Lieutenant Kinkead who was killed while attempting to break the world air speed record over the Solent in 1928, is buried in the church-yard.

Dibden

All Saints

The church at Dibden, also called All Saints, was the first church in Britain to be damaged by enemy action. Many treasures were lost including 14th century stained glass from the chancel and communion rails made of yew with twisted baluster shafts dating from 1660. The 13th century font was damaged when the bells fell from the tower but has since been faithfully restored.

The origins of the church are uncertain but the list of rectors starts with Master Ralph in 1262 and the chancel arch, with its unusual rounded shafts, dates from the 13th century. The low and battlemented tower was built in 1884. The church was lovingly restored and consecrated in 1955 — 'A Joyful Resurrection'.

The vault of the Lisle family of Moyles Court, Ellingham lies beneath the chancel. The Lisles were associated, by marriage, to the ownership of Dibden Manor. The Manor was set alight by the same incendiary bomb that hit the church.

Lymington
St. Thomas

The long and turbulent history of the parish church of Lymington began around 1250 when it was built in the form of a Latin Cross. The church was repeatedly ravaged by the French in raids along the coast from the 14th to the 16th centuries and in 1660 was gutted and occupied by Puritan soldiers in the Civil War. After each sacking the church was rebuilt and expanded in the style of the period.

The tower and cupola was added after the restoration of Charles II and the interior was given its classical structure during the Napoleonic Wars when the three galleries were supported by Tuscan columns.

The parish register of St. Thomas's records the baptism of Caroline Ann Bowles the New Forest poet and second wife of Poet Laureate, Robert Southey who were married in Boldre church. Caroline Bowles was born in Lymington and is buried in the churchyard. Her tomb is set between the east and west walls.

It is a short walk down the High Street to Lymington Quay where, at high tide, the creek abounds with boats and there are fine views across the Solent to the Isle of Wight.

Milford-on-Sea
All Saints

The ancient and beautiful parish church of Milford, which has its beginnings in Norman times also carries features of the Early English, Decorated and Perpendicular styles.

As you enter the church you are facing the two arches of the south arcade which are of the late Norman period and still bear the 800 year old carvings.

It is thought that the small window in the south lean-to was at one time a door used to smuggle in beer for the bell-ringers.

In the churchyard are two flat gravestones lying north to south instead of the usual east to west. These are said to be the graves of two suicides. On one is the inscription '... after witnessing the departure of all most dear to him, of a wife and many daughters, he *departed himself* from this world on the ...'

In the town, at the corner of Cornwallis Road and Victoria Road, is the oldest pillar-box in Hampshire dating from about 1856 and with a vertical posting slot.

From nearby Keyhaven boat trips can be taken to Hurst Castle.

About the Artist

Barry Peckham has lived all his life in the New Forest. His art reflects his love of the Forest, its customs and inhabitants.

He works in most media; oils, watercolour, pastel, pen and ink and zinc and copper plate etching.

Preferring as he does to work directly from the subject, he can often be seen working outside at his easel, no matter what the weather.

His work was first shown in London in 1974 and he is now a regular exhibitor at such venues as the Royal Academy, Royal Institute of Oil Painters, Royal Society of Marine Artists.

He is a member of the Society of Equestrian Artists.

About the Author

Georgina Peckham is an active conservationist, book-dealer and free-lance writer. Although she has travelled in three continents her feeling for the New Forest, in which she was born and still lives, is evident in her prose. This is her first book.